GLENCORSE PRIMARY SCHOOL
MILTON BRIDGE
PENICUIK

RECEIVED

2 8 APR 1998

LIVING FOR THE *FUTURE*

WORLD POPULATION

Nance Fyson

FRANKLIN WATTS
NEW YORK • LONDON • SYDNEY

Most of our everyday activities, whether turning on a light or taking a trip in a car, use up some of the earth's resources. These resources will not last forever, yet we continue to need and use them in our daily lives.

In June 1992, the largest ever political meeting in history was held — the United Nations Conference on Environment and Development (UNCED), or the 'Earth Summit'. Politicians, environmental experts and many others gathered together to discuss the challenge that humanity faces as we move towards the twenty-first century. How can we live our lives in a way that suits us, but without using up the resources that our children in turn will need to live their lives?

Agenda 21 is the document that was produced as a result of the Earth Summit. It sets out a practical plan for every nation to follow to achieve 'sustainable development'. This means not only allowing us to live the lives we want to lead, but allowing everyone else to live a comfortable life, while also protecting our environment for future generations.

© 1998 Franklin Watts
96 Leonard Street
London
EC2A 4RH

Franklin Watts Australia
14 Mars Road
Lane Cove
NSW 2066

ISBN 0 7496 2855 3
Dewey Decimal Classification Number 304.6
A CIP catalogue record for this book is available from the British Library

Series editor: Helen Lanz
Series designer: Kirstie Billingham
Designer: Simon Borrough
Picture research: Sue Mennell
Consultant: Niall Marriott, a founder of Living Earth Foundation and consultant in environmental, community and educational issues

The Publishers would like to thank Jeremy Hamand of the International Planned Parenthood Federation for his helpful suggestions.

Printed in the United Kingdom

CONTENTS

Can you imagine more than 5,900 million people? That is the number alive in the world today. By the year 2050, there could be nearly twice as many people on this planet!

PEOPLE TODAY

INCREASING NUMBERS

Many centuries ago, there were far fewer people – and the population grew much more slowly than today. Gradually, however, better health care and cleaner living conditions helped more people live to an older age. More of the babies that were born survived. At the same time, people found ways of growing larger amounts of food to support the growing population. The number of people on earth started to increase very quickly.

As people live longer, the death rate (the number of people who die per thousand) goes down. Unless parents have fewer children, which lowers the birth rate (the number of babies born per thousand), populations rise.

Today, three babies are born in the world every second (left); more people are also living longer (above), so the population is rising rapidly.

THE WORLD DIVIDE

Although people do live longer now, and more babies do survive throughout the world, people are not spread evenly across the globe. Some countries are much more crowded than others. About one-quarter of the world's people live in the richer countries of the world, such as Britain, the United States and Australia. In these countries, women have, on average, 1.8 children each.

Australia is one of the world's least crowded countries. Eighteen million people live on a continent about the size of the United States.

There are big differences between the world's rich and poor. Over 1,000 million people live in severe poverty.

The root causes of poverty are hunger, illiteracy, inadequate medical care, unemployment and population pressures.

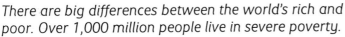

More than three-quarters of the world's population live in the poorer countries of Asia, Africa and Latin America. The population is growing fastest in these poorer parts of the world, where, on average, women have between three and six children each.

The rate of the world's population growth has fallen over the last 20 years, but the number of babies born each year has increased — it is now over 80 million. (That is like adding a country with Britain's population every nine months!) This is because the larger population of the 1970s is now reaching maturity, and starting to have children. By the year 2025, it is expected that there will be 2,200 million more people in the world than there are today. But while the number of people increases, the earth does not get any bigger.

Today 94% of all babies are being born in the poor countries of Asia, Africa and Latin America.

USING RESOURCES

INCREASING DEMANDS

Growing numbers of people make increasing demands on the earth and its resources. Everyone needs to be fed, have access to water for drinking and washing and to have a home. Food, water and building materials are all natural resources that come from our environment.

Some resources, such as energy from the sun, are 'renewable' because they do not run out. Other resources, such as oil and coal, are called 'non-renewable'. They run down as we use them and cannot be replaced.

Developed countries have only about one-fifth of the world's people, but with their many labour-saving devices such as washing machines, they use about four-fifths of the world's resources.

Resources such as rainforests are under great threat. They are being run down rapidly – especially in poorer, tropical countries. As the population increases, there is a greater need for more wood – to be burnt as fuel or to be used for building and making other products. Additionally, as people need more food, forests are cleared to make way for more farm land.

The loss of forests upsets the climate, soil and rainfall, and destroys the habitats of animals.

CASE STUDY

FEEDING THE WORLD

THE ISSUES AT STAKE

Until 1985, world food supplies grew in line with the added numbers of people. The world had enough grain stored then to feed everyone for 104 days. But by 1996, there was only enough grain stored to feed everyone for 51 days. Production of cereals, such as wheat and rice, is now lower per person than at any time since 1975.

The poorest countries are most at risk. In Africa, food production per person fell by one-fifth from 1975 to 1995. A 1996 World Disaster Report said that over 750 million people in the world do not have enough basic food.

One-third of the world's children do not have the healthy food they need.

POURING OUT WASTES

People also use the earth to get rid of wastes – solids, liquids and gases. Human waste pours into rivers and seas, polluting our waterways. One of the biggest problems is waste gases – these harm forests, plants and animal-life, and affect the climate.

New York City's Fresh Kills landfill site receives 100,000 tonnes of refuse from the city each week.

Our wastes are not only what we throw away. There are also by-products, such as fumes from cars and industry. When fuels, such as coal and wood, are burnt, gases called sulphur dioxide and nitrogen oxides are made. These gases mix with water droplets in the atmosphere, or air. This then falls as acid rain which kills trees and fish, and erodes our ancient buildings. The greater the number of people, the greater the amount of waste and pollution we produce.

La Paz, Bolivia, is one of the fastest growing cities in the world.

TAKING UP SPACE

People also use the earth by taking up space. With more and more people, there are also more houses, factories, roads and buildings. More people means less room for the natural environment – wildlife, plants and forests.

If the number of people in the world were to rise to 11,500 million, we would need an extra 12.5 million sq km of land for farms and cities. This is nearly double the land which is set aside and protected today for wildlife. It is an area about two-fifths the size of Africa.

The 57 million people added to developed countries in the 1990s are doing more damage to the earth's atmosphere and oceans than the 911 million people being added in developing nations.

Space is becoming more and more valuable as the number of people in the world increases.

CASE STUDY

BRITAIN

THE ISSUES AT STAKE

Britain has a low rate of new babies being born now — but it is one of the world's most crowded countries. The density of people (the number of people per hectare) is high.

The limited space, high density of people, and rapidly changing lifestyles means that more and more pressure is put on reserved areas such as national parks. Wild animals, plants and their habitats suffer as areas are cleared for buildings and roads.

Areas of natural beauty suffer as they are filled with many visitors, or are used for development.

Government officials, conservationists, scientists and many others have come to realize that the earth's resources will not last forever. Increasing numbers of people obviously have an impact on the environment. Links have been made between the growing population, the rise in poverty and damage to the environment. Since numbers are expected to keep rising well into the 21st century, officials are concerned about the future.

More people, more pollution.

AGENDA 21 – A PLAN FOR THE FUTURE

Officials gather at the Earth Summit in Rio de Janeiro.

In 1992, people from all over the world met in Rio de Janeiro, Brazil, at a Conference on Environment and Development (UNCED), or the 'Earth Summit'. It was the biggest meeting ever held, and it was called to discuss the issues of how people could live comfortably, but without destroying the environment.

LIVING RESPONSIBLY

A plan of action called 'Agenda 21' was set up. This says that the world must develop in a way that is 'sustainable'. People must live responsibly, and use the earth's resources carefully, to allow people in the future to live reasonable lives as well. If people today are greedy and careless, the earth will not be much of a place tomorrow.

Here are some of the most important aims of Agenda 21 that relate to world population:

- people need access to education and training to promote employment and reduce poverty
- governments and local communities must provide adequate health care, with family planning services
- people should have access to decent housing
- poorer, developing countries should be supported by richer, developed nations
- each nation must establish the maximum number of people it can provide for and keep its population below this level
- each nation must look at population trends in order to set out a long-term plan of action

CASE STUDY

CAIRO, EGYPT

AN INTERNATIONAL CONFERENCE ON POPULATION

In 1994, people from many different nations met at an International Conference on Population and Development (ICPD). The conference made a plan to try and hold the world's population to 8,500 million people by the year 2025 – and 9,800 million people by 2050.

The conference looked at why some people still have big families in order to be able to put forward some practical ideas to encourage these people to have smaller families. For example, giving women better education and chances for jobs outside the home is part of the plan. Women are then likely to want fewer children.

Women discuss the issues raised at the conference on population.

There are many reasons why people have large families. These reasons need to be understood before any action can be taken to try and reduce the number of children parents have, and so reduce the population throughout the world.

In most developed countries, people are able to claim benefits while they are looking for work.

WHY LARGE FAMILIES?

In many countries, people earn very low wages. In some countries, particularly developing nations, there is little or no social security. (This is money, raised through taxes, that governments use to support people who are sick and unable to work, those who are unemployed, or people who are too old to work.) Where there is no social security, families must look after themselves.

Large families are more able to support themselves than smaller ones. In countries such as India, children often work to bring in extra money. Children also help with daily chores – carrying water, collecting firewood and minding farm animals – so the more children there are, the more security there is for the family.

Children work to bring in extra money for the family.

A MATTER OF SURVIVAL

There are still countries where many babies and young children die young from diseases. In the poorest parts of Africa, one out of five children dies before the age of five. People may have large families to be sure some children will live to be adults.

FAMILY PLANNING

Today, more and more people use 'family planning' methods, or birth control, to have fewer children. This includes advice and medical support to prevent people from producing babies by using contraceptive devices, such as 'the pill' or condoms.

In many parts of Africa, families are faced with war and famine. The death rate among children is high.

However, people in remote areas, or people from particular religious or traditional backgrounds, may not have access to 'family planning' services, and so have less control over the number of children they have.

The United Nations 1997 State of World Population found that 120 – 150 million women would use family planning if they had access to information and services.

It has been shown that where people have greater access to education and employment, the population decreases because people *want* fewer children.

In most developed countries, birth control is seen as a right.

- improve rural living and working conditions to prevent migration to the cities
- prevent urban sprawl on to farm land
- provide more basic housing
- provide basic education and training

Education is an important tool in controlling population size.

A SECURE FUTURE

Unemployment and underemployment is a growing world problem. As the world's population increases, there is growing pressure on the number of jobs available. People's ability to earn a living to support themselves and their families is closely linked with their standard of living. And people's standard of living has an impact on the environment.

'Too much population growth increases environmental and social stress, reducing the quality of life.'

AGENDA 21

FROM COUNTRY TO CITY

In Europe, many people began moving from farms and into cities in the late 19th and early 20th centuries. The same kind of move is now happening in the poorer countries of Asia, Africa and Latin America. Some people leave rural areas because growing populations mean that there is too little land left to farm. Also, more machinery means less work is available.

Some farm land is too poor for crops, but there are not enough alternative jobs, besides farming, for people in rural areas.

Many of these people are being drawn to the cities hoping for a better life – but this is a big problem. As more people flock to cities, there are less jobs available here, as well. Additionally, there is often not enough housing, clean water or other services for all who come. People build makeshift homes on any bit of land they can find.

The population of cities in poorer countries, such as Dhaka, Bangladesh, increased four times over the years 1950 to 1990.

UNHEALTHY LIVING

In some cities, like Nairobi, in Kenya, and Dhaka, in Bangladesh, over three-quarters of homes have been built without permission. These makeshift homes, or shanty towns, are often unhealthy, with no proper facilities or sanitation. They also use up precious land on the outskirts of towns and cities, reducing the area for growing crops and food.

The United Nations Food and Agriculture Organization runs many projects, such as this one in Mozambique, to enable small communities to support themselves.

IMPROVING CONDITIONS

'Poverty causes environmental damage – and the damage in turn causes poverty'

AGENDA 21

Governments need to put policies into place to encourage people to stay in rural areas. This means that they need to improve job opportunities, so local people can earn a living. This would help slow the drift of people to cities.

In poorer countries, many parents have large numbers of children to improve their own prospects in old age. Often, young children go out to work to earn money to help support the family.

Improving people's education and skills is one way to solve this problem. By being better educated, people have more choices. They are more qualified to do a greater variety of work. Throughout the world, where people are better educated and more able to support themselves, their standard of living tends to go up and the size of families tends to go down.

Many children in poorer countries work to help their parents. Laws try to protect children from working long hours in poor conditions.

ZERO POPULATION GROWTH

In developed countries, population growth has slowed down. People are having fewer children and lowering the birth rate. 'Zero population growth' – where just enough babies are being born to maintain population levels – happened first in East Germany in 1969. By 1997, Germany's population rate was still low.

By 1997 in Britain, the number of babies born was just below 1.7 children per married woman.

16

THE NEED FOR EDUCATION

Pakistan has an average of 5.6 children for every married woman. At the start of the 1990s, only about 12% of women aged between 15 and 49 years were using birth control. While four-fifths of Pakistan's population know about family planning, many families are still large. Part of the reason is that many women there still have little education.

In traditional communities, where men are the decision-makers, changing the role of women can be hard.

'More education, especially of girls, will help to reduce further the size of families.'

AGENDA 21

EDUCATION FOR ALL

In much of the world, girls have less schooling than boys. In Latin America, less than half of girls go to secondary school. In South Asia, only 28% of girls have secondary education. In the parts of Africa south of the Sahara Desert, only 14% of girls go to secondary school.

Yet in all countries, women who have seven or more years of education are likely to marry more than five years later than those who do not receive this length of schooling. They are also likely to have two or three fewer children.

Where women have received education and training, they can choose not to have a family but to have a job. This car workshop in Bangladesh employs three women and four men.

A WAY FORWARD

Governments need to encourage parents to have smaller families – and improving education for all is one way forward. If girls are allowed more education, they are likely to marry later and have fewer children. If allowed to have some secondary schooling, a woman is ten times more likely to use family planning.

In Europe, only 10% of women marry before the age of 20. In Africa, 40% of women marry before they are 20 years old.

(Above) With women marrying at an older age, the number of new babies being born tends to be lower. In Italy, where this wedding is taking place, birth rates are very low.

The relationship between education and the use of family planning is an important one. While education is a valuable tool in the bid to slow the population growth, it is one that works slowly. It needs to be used alongside other methods of population control.

Now, in countries such as Senegal, adult literacy classes for women are encouraged.

Countries with over 100 million people (UN estimated figures, 1997)

China	1,236 million
India	970 million
United States	267 million
Indonesia	204 million
Brazil	160 million
Russian Federation	147 million
Pakistan	138 million
Japan	126 million
Bangladesh	122 million
Nigeria	107 million

THE VALUE OF EDUCATION

China, India, Indonesia, Brazil, Pakistan, Bangladesh, Nigeria, Mexico and Egypt together have half the world's people. In these nine countries, nearly three-quarters of the people cannot read and write. In 1994, the governments of these nine countries made plans for better education programmes, recognizing that this was a way to help slow population growth.

CASE STUDY

A WORLDWIDE TREND

LATER MOTHERHOOD

More and more women are opting to have children later on in life, if they opt to have any at all. In Britain, the rate of births for women in their early thirties is increasing, and the rate of births for women in their early 20s decreasing. Research in the 1997 edition of Population Trends, published by the Office of National Statistics, indicated that many women are waiting until they have established their careers before starting a family. One in four women are choosing not to have any children at all, compared with one in ten in the early 1960s.

It is now common for women in many countries to combine having a family with having a job. This often means women choose to have children later in life.

CONTROLLING FAMILY SIZE

Family planning leads to better health and well-being. Women and children are healthier if there is at least two years between the birth of one child and the next. Since the early 1970s, more and more women are saying openly that they want fewer children. Today, more women want control over the number of children they have and when they have them.

The National Health Service in the UK ensures free access to birth control.

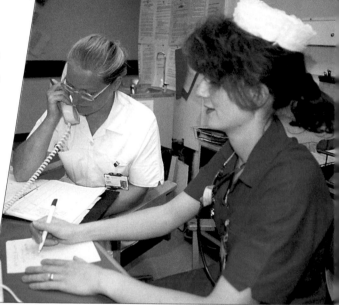

Governments can help couples have more information about and access to family planning services.
In Britain, for example, birth control was made free on the National Health Service in 1974. By contrast, until 1974, Brazil encouraged larger families. Women were having, on average, nearly six children each. But by the 1980s, family planning in Brazil was being encouraged and women were having an average of three children each.

Women who want to pursue a career need to control when they have their children, and so family planning is crucial.

Large families are still common in many countries in Latin America. However, Chile, Colombia and Costa Rica have lowered their birth rates by nearly a third since the 1960s.

In 1967, family planning services in Indonesia set up a programme for better health, welfare and education. 'Two children are enough' was the slogan used on radio, television and posters. People were even given rice as a reward for using contraceptives. The campaign proved very successful. From an average of six children per woman in the early 1960s, the average in the mid-1990s was less than three children per woman. Only about a tenth of married women used contraceptives in the early 1960s, but over half do now.

CASE STUDY

THAILAND

ENCOURAGING SMALLER FAMILIES

Thailand is one success story in the bid to encourage smaller families. Years ago, the King gave a gold medal to couples with ten children. Big families were encouraged.
Over the last 30 years, there has been a change. Couples are now encouraged to have fewer children. Only 15% of couples used family planning methods in 1969 – but nearly 70% used birth control by the 1990s. Thailand has also done much to improve education for women. Nearly as many girls are in secondary school as boys.

In Thailand, smaller families are rewarded with goods.

CULTURE AND COMMUNITIES

We are all part of different communities and cultures and follow different religions and traditions. This means that population control is more difficult to promote in some areas than others.

THE LOSS OF LAND

Africa is one of the least crowded continents – but the population is growing faster here than anywhere else. This is a problem because there is not enough food, housing, jobs and clean water for all the extra people.

The increasing population has dramatic effects on the environment as more land is cleared for building or for farming. This results in the loss of topsoil – the valuable soil that is rich in nutrients needed for crops to grow. In some areas, this soil is not very deep. As trees are removed, the soil dries out and blows away in the wind.

As the population in Africa increases resources, such as water and land, suffer.

In Africa, the loss of topsoil — and the resulting increase of desert size — is making the land less good for growing food. In 36 out of 45 African countries south of the Sahara Desert, food production has not kept up with the growing population over the last 20 years.

Growing hedges on the steep soil slopes, such as here in the Cameroon, is an important device in preventing soil from being washed away. Then communities can strive to feed their own population.

Education means choices for these Kenyan school children.

A SIGN OF MANHOOD

Women in Kenya, still have, on average, over six children each. Efforts are being made to encourage family planning. In the mid-1970s, only about 6% of Kenyan women used modern birth control — but this is now up to nearly 30%.

One of the difficulties in Kenya, and other countries, is to encourage men to care about having smaller families. Men in many cultures see having a lot of children as a sign of manhood. In some countries, women still have little power to choose.

The fact that women in some cultures still follow very traditional roles was recognized at the Earth Summit. Some women may not have access to education or family planning services; they may not be allowed to make any decisions of their own. Agenda 21 states in order to bring down population growth rates, women should be allowed more control over their own lives. Men need to be made part of this process in order to raise their awareness of women's changing roles. This includes encouraging them to share responsibility for family planning.

Women's groups, such as this one in Bangladesh, help to build the confidence of local women.

TAKING RESPONSIBILITY

In 1984, the Health Education Council in Britain started a campaign called 'Men Too'. A poster showed a 'pregnant man' with the caption: 'You'd be more careful if you became pregnant'. This campaign was launched to educate men to take more responsibility for using contraceptives. Other countries, such as Sri Lanka and those in the Caribbean and India, have encouraged men to show more support for family planning, too.

24

In Sri Lanka, field workers visit rural villages specifically to inform men about family planning.

CONFLICTING OPINIONS

Some values and traditions brought communities into conflict with the aims of Agenda 21. The issues of contraception and abortion caused many difficulties when the plans to control the population were discussed. Strong feelings about abortion, held by the Catholic Church and representatives of the United States, meant that the chapters on population control were not as detailed as they perhaps could have been.

Abortion is a very controversial issue in many countries, especially the United States.

CASE STUDY

ITALY

CHANGING TRENDS

Italy has no government policy on population. Most people follow the Catholic religion. While the Pope, who heads the Roman Catholic Church, has encouraged larger families, most families are actually small. Surprisingly, Italy now has the lowest rate of new babies in the world.

Italian couples tend to be older when they first marry – usually about the age of 25. There are few babies born outside marriages (6% compared to 25% in the UK). It is now more common for women to work outside the home, and it is also easier than before for them to get modern methods of birth control.

Plans for controlling population levels need to work alongside different beliefs and values.

AGENDA 21 aims to:

- encourage governments to adopt population policies
- encourage each nation to assess its maximum population capacity
- ensure each nation keeps its population below its capacity

POPULATION POLICIES

Sometimes, governments have encouraged bigger populations. In the early 1980s, nearly 20 countries still had policies encouraging larger families. In Bulgaria, child allowances increased for the second and additional children in a family. France used to give medals to mothers with four or more children – large families are still generously provided for by the state.

IT IS BETTER TO HAVE ONE CHILD ONLY

只生一个孩子

Posters like this have encouraged family planning. Slogans such as 'small families have more to spend' are used.

In ancient Rome, about 40 BC, Julius Caesar gave rewards to parents with large families.

But pressure is mounting for each government to reduce its country's population and to formalize policies relating to population control. Agenda 21 asks governments to assess how many people their countries can provide for – and to keep the population below this level. Some governments now discourage large families through taxes and other penalties. India and some countries in Africa, for example, offer tax benefits for smaller families.

ONE-CHILD POLICY

China and India probably have the most well-known population policies in the world. These countries together have about a third of the world's people and what happens in each is very important to the world's population.

From 1949 to 1969, the Chinese population grew quickly – 260 million people were added to the population, nearly the size of the United States today. In 1979, the government started a 'One-Child Policy'. Couples are given benefits in housing and education, for example, for having only one child. There are exceptions to the rule; rural families can now have a second child if the first is a boy.

The 'One-Child Policy' policy has helped to lower the birth rate, but a number of problems have arisen. Many parents want a boy and are unhappy if the first child is a girl.

It took China 4,000 years to reach a population of 100 million. In just another 80 years, that number had doubled.

CASE STUDY

INDIA

A LONG-TERM POLICY

In 1952, India became the first country in the world to have an official population policy. In the 1970s, the country tried sterilizing millions of people so they could not bear children. 'Family planning' became unpopular because of this. The government realized it was being too heavy-handed. After the population conference in Cairo, India changed its policy, moving away from fertility targets. Complete health care programmes were offered, including reproductive health and sex education.

By taking care of social needs through health care, it is felt that population levels will stabilize themselves.

It is not enough just to tell people to have smaller families. Governments must help people gain a better standard of living and feel more secure. More general education for women and better chances to gain work will help. Improving the health of mothers and babies can lead to smaller families.

Changing the role of women worldwide is key to tackling the population issue.

TOO MANY?

The United Nations thinks there will be about 9.4 billion people on earth by the year 2050. That is twice the population of 1987. The number might then go higher. No one can know for sure.

'Communities need to develop their own policies for sustainable population growth.'

AGENDA 21

The growing world population is adding to pollution of the atmosphere, rivers and oceans. Forests are becoming scarcer and land is becoming poorer. Holding down the number of people on its own will not solve all the problems of the environment. But controlling the population is part of world conservation. The number of people affects the quality of life on earth.

As populations rise, demands on the countryside grow.

Social and economic changes can help make parents *want* smaller families. Modern methods of birth control give people a way of being able to *choose* to have fewer children. In the early 1960s, only about one in ten couples in the world were using family planning. The world average of the number of children per couple was 6.1. By 1997, 56% of couples were using family planning. The world average of children per couple was down to only 3.0.

People's social and economic needs influence their lifestyles. By meeting these needs, birthrates may level out of their own accord.

Agenda 21 gave governments real goals to try to lower the populations of their countries. Governments have been asked to work out sustainable development plans to offer solutions to housing and employment issues, and to provide health care and family planning services. They have been asked to look at past and present population trends in order to plan for trends in the future.

But Agenda 21 also asks that people in every village, town and city take responsibility for the way they live their lives today. Only then will the people of tomorrow have a choice in how they live their lives.

World population is not only growing, it is also changing. Young people have usually out-numbered old people. But by the year 2025, there are likely to be more people aged over 60 than there are people under 15 years old.

GLOSSARY

abortion: an operation which takes place in the early stages of pregnancy, preventing the pregnancy from continuing.

Agenda 21: plan of action made at the Earth Summit in 1992 in an effort to preserve the earth's resources.

atmosphere: the different gases that surround the earth.

birth control: using devices, such as 'the pill' or condoms, or not having sexual intercourse at certain times each month, so that a woman is less likely to become pregnant.

birth rate: the number of babies born for every 1000 people in a population.

condom: a rubber sheath placed over a man's penis to stop sperm being released, and so preventing him from making a woman pregnant.

conservation: the protection of the environment and earth's resources.

contraceptive: a means of deliberately preventing pregnancy.

death rate: number of people dying for every 1000 people in a population.

density: how crowded a country is with people.

developed country: a country that relies on money from industry and in which factories provide more jobs than agriculture.

developing country: a country that relies on money from agriculture, rather than on manufacturing goods for export, for example.

environment: all the conditions that surround us, such as the air, the soil and habitats of animals, including people.

family planning: this can be a service, source of advice or a decision taken by a couple to limit the number of children they have – planning the number and deciding on the space between births.

income tax: money deducted from a person's salary and paid to the government in order to fund services for the good of the community, such as putting up buildings, providing education and so on.

literacy: the ability to read and write.

maternity benefits: payments or services, such as health visits, for pregnant women and new mothers.

migration: the movement of people from one place to another.

pill: 'the pill' is a general term referring to the different types of contraceptive pill, taken by mouth, to prevent pregnancy.

population: the number of people in a specific area.

resource: a stock or supply of a material. Coal, oil and gas are all natural resources.

social security: support from the state, or government, in the form of money or help with housing, health care and so on.

sterilization: an operation available to a man or woman so that the woman is unable to become pregnant.

sustainable development: to be able to maintain lifestyles or preserve resources over a long period of time.

trend: a repeated pattern or the tendency of something to keep happening.

FURTHER INFORMATION

Birth Control Trust (BCT)
27-35 Mortimer Street
London W1N 7RJ, UK
Tel: 0171 580 9360

International Planned Parenthood Federation (IPPF)
Regent's College
Inner Circle
Regent's Park
London NW1 4NS, UK
Tel: 0171 487 7900

Population Concern
178-202 Great Portland Street
London W1N 5TB, UK
Tel: 0171 631 1546

United Nations Information Centre UK
18 Buckingham Gate
London SW1E 6LB, UK
Tel: 0171 630 1981

UNICEF UK
55 Lincoln's Inn Fields
London WC2A 3NB, UK
Tel: 0171 405 5592

Family Planning Australia
PO Box 26
Deakin West
ACT 2600
AUSTRALIA
Tel: 06 285 1244

UNICEF Australia
9th Floor/55 Bathurst Street
Sydney, NSW 2000
AUSTRALIA
Tel: 02 9290 2099

United Nations Information Centre Australia
125 York Street
Sydney, NSW 2000
AUSTRALIA
Tel: 02 9283 1144

World Health Organization
PO Box 404
Abbotsford,
Victoria 3076
AUSTRALIA
Tel: 03 9417 5361

INDEX